Creative Romance

Creative Romance

DOUG FIELDS

HARVEST HOUSE PUBLISHERS
Eugene, Oregon 97402

Published in association with the literary agency of Alive Communications, Colorado Springs, Colorado.

CREATIVE ROMANCE

Copyright © 1991 by Doug Fields
Published by Harvest House Publishers
Eugene, Oregon 97402

Library of Congress Cataloging-in-Publication Data

Fields, Doug, 1962-
    Creative romance / Doug Fields.
    ISBN 0-89081-880-0
    1. Marriage—United States—Humor.   2. Interpersonal rela-
tions—Humor.   I. Title.
HQ734.F428   1991   91-9738
646.7'8—dc20   CIP

To my wonderful wife, Cathy,
whose love for me ignites my romance
and inspires my creativity.
I love being with you!

Contents

♥

Introduction

1. Dating Your Mate 13

2. Celebrating Marriage 23

3. Keeping Romance in Marriage 33

4. Romancing...Creatively 41

5. Elements of a Romantic Date 51

6. 200 Romantic Things You Could Easily Do ... 61

7. Play with a Purpose 73

8. 14 Creative Date Strategies 81

9. Romance at Home 93

10. Creative Gift Giving 103

11. Taking Romance on the Road 115

12. The Power of Words 127

13. Creative Encouragement 137

Introduction

♥

I enjoy talking with people who love their spouses and consider their marriages to be quality unions. I usually find that the common denominator behind their happiness is the principle of working hard at their marital relationships. Such people will tell you that good marriages take time. They will also assure you that there is no quick fix idea you can buy and no new, slick technique you can employ to immediately relieve the pain of a struggling relationship. Happily married couples provide encouragement and hope by reminding us that marriage can be the most intimate and satisfying relation we can have with another human. But good marriages don't just happen.

This book was written to help couples of all age groups regardless of their current circumstances. This isn't a book filled with answers. Instead it is packed with encouragement and ideas which can help make your marriage either a little or a lot better than it is right now.

The strength of your marriage depends on the choices you make to improve it. My hope is that you will read this book from cover to cover and allow the ideas to be a springboard from which you start taking action. Don't leave *Creative Romance* lying around with the hope your spouse will read it and "shape up." Begin with yourself! Start making choices to enjoy one of God's greatest gifts to you...your spouse.

Though this book has one author, several people played significant roles by reading the manuscript and contributing comments and ideas. Special thanks to Jennifer Hughes-Adams, Loreen Leake, Scott Rachels, Todd Temple, Rand Tucker, Noel Veale, Linda Vujnov, Dan York, and my incredible assistant, Karen Page.

I am grateful to my editor, Lela Gilbert, who pushed me to write more than ideas and to broaden my thinking to encompass the reality of pain.

I also want to thank a few of my good friends whose love for their wives has been an encouragement and model to me: Jim Burns, Lou Douros, Jeff Genoway, Alan Smith, and Doug Webster—thank you, guys.

Dating
Your Mate

♥

1

I love to watch people. My wife, Cathy, and I were recently at a resort. While lounging beside a huge swimming pool, we watched a hundred-plus people tanning, swimming, playing, reading, and otherwise enjoying themselves. Because I was concentrating on this book, I focused my attention on the various couples around the pool.

As far as I could see, the pairs having the best time weren't the married ones. As a matter of fact, most of the married couples appeared rather bored. If they were having fun with each other, you'd never have known it by looking at them. We watched one couple in their seventies playing around in the water, giggling, splashing, and enjoying one another immensely. I assumed, because of their age, that they were married. But we soon learned it wasn't so—they, too, were just "dating"!

*M*en and Women Are Different (In case you didn't know!)
♥

I realize that my poolside observations do not constitute a scientific study of marriage. But my simple conclusion is this: Many couples become bored and disinterested once they are married. And this point of view is reinforced by my daily encounters with married couples for whom dating and romance are all but nonexistent.

For years, I've spoken to groups on the subject of creative dating. And the one response I continually hear is, "Those ideas you presented sound like a lot of fun—but I'm married!" I've heard this so many times I'm beginning to believe there's a clause on the marriage license stating, "Once married you shall no longer date. Furthermore, if you decide to do anything resembling a date it shall be called 'going-out' and shall never be too exciting!"

If you can empathize with the plight of a partner in an uneventful marriage, or if you have at times found your marriage void of romance, you need to understand three simple truths:

1. You're not alone.

2. You can be more romantic very easily.

3. This book will help.

It's your attitude and your willingness to change yourself and your behavior that can make the difference in your marital circumstances. With the right spirit and motivation, this book can help strengthen a good marriage as well as encourage a troubled one. The ideas presented herein are fun, silly, and even outlandish. A few ideas are designed to bring out your childlike spirit and to encourage playful interaction. Some ideas will inspire you toward greater depth in your relationship, while others may make you shudder. Please realize that these are only suggestions— meant to serve as the icing highlighting a multi-layered cake.

The secret to sharing a good marriage can never be a bunch of clever ideas anyway. If you're counting on my suggestions to solve your troubles, you're going to be disappointed. There isn't a quick fix to any marriage, no matter how creative the remedy might be. You can't skip the main ingredients of a recipe and expect the icing to make up for the bad taste and texture of the cake. Good marriages don't function that way, either. They take time and energy.

Unfortunately, many couples have lost the spark they shared before they married and have replaced it with a humdrum routine. Dating and romancing your spouse can change those patterns, and can be a lot of fun, but will require some hard work. Planning and energy are imperative for making good times happen.

Is it worth the trouble? I'm convinced that the lack of dating and romance in marriage is one of the major causes of broken relationships. Marriages usually don't collapse overnight. They become bankrupt gradually because they lack daily deposits of love, communication, and affirmation.

I recently heard a local congressman tell a reporter that he is willing to do "anything" to help rebuild Kuwait in the aftermath of its terrible destruction. I thought this was an interesting comment. Not long ago, this same man allowed his marriage to fall apart. The physical devastation of Kuwait will be repaired within a few years. But once a marriage relationship is destroyed, it can rarely be renovated. "Preventative maintenance" takes ongoing work—work that must be done sooner, not later.

*S*uccessful Marriages Require Our Best Efforts
♥

I find very few people who have trouble agreeing that a good marriage requires hard work. But most people struggle and get discouraged when they try to explain their own lack of dating and romance. There are countless excuses guaranteed to keep you from taking action when it comes to dating your mate. I know all about them—I've thought of several myself:

♥ | What are we going to do with the children?
♥ | I don't have enough time.
♥ | Dating costs too much money.
♥ | There's plenty to do at home.
♥ | I'm too tired.
♥ | There's nothing to do where we live.
♥ | We can't ever get good baby-sitters.
♥ | It's too cold outside.
♥ | I've got too much to do around the house.

It's true. We can always think of excuses to avoid doing certain things. I can think of ten reasons for not getting out of bed in the morning, and another five for not filling my car with gasoline. I can make all the excuses I want to, but eventually the pressures of reality will force me into action. The urgency of life tells me I'd better get out of bed and get gas in my car. Otherwise I'll never make it to work, I'll get myself fired, and I'll end up without enough money for survival! I'm forced to do what I should, regardless of my excuses. That's reality.

But as far as my marriage is concerned, the consequences of my excuses aren't nearly as tangible or immediate. If I don't take Cathy out on Friday night, so what? Life will go on. I'll still be employed. I'll still be able to afford gas. I'm not forced to make any special effort toward our relationship because there appears to be no urgency. I can continue not making deposits for a long time before my marriage account dries up.

You don't need to be a rocket-scientist to figure out that this sort of attitude lies behind the rapid deterioration of marriages. Our nation's divorce rate is phenomenal. If it continues at the present rate, we won't have any families left by the year 2008!

If you want to add life to your marriage, perhaps even save its life, you'd better do whatever it takes to bring romance and dating back into the picture. As I said, there's no quick fix. But if you're willing to make the proper investments, you'll find great rewards. So—in the face of all the excuses, let's take a look at five important ways you will benefit from dating your spouse.

𝒟ating Strengthens Your Relationship

♥

Relationships are strengthened through time spent together, honest communication, and positive memories.

Dating provides all of these. Dating builds up marriages and helps solidify their foundations. Enduring relationships aren't constructed out of fleeting emotions and occasional passion. They are solidly built on quality time spent together, each partner investing in the other.

Cathy and I have a date-night once a week. We don't necessarily make every date a "creative date." But almost without exception, our time of shared experience and intimacy brings us closer together. It's not always easy and inexpensive to find a baby-sitter, but we place high priority on our weekly dates. And the value they add to our marriage can't be measured in financial terms.

*D*ating
Enriches Life
♥

Life was given to us by our Creator to be lived to its fullest. And He gave us a great playground we affectionately call "Earth" to use and enjoy while we have the opportunity. Setting time aside to enjoy one another is not only pleasing to God but enriches the quality of our lives. You are bound to be a much better husband or wife when you invest time in your marriage, giving it higher priority than such things as the television set or the PTA or the office or church activities or the golf course.

*D*ating Creates
Positive Memories
♥

Memories recall significant expressions of the past. Quality relationships are rich in positive memories.

Since our world does a good job of dispensing negative experiences, it's up to us to do an even better job of providing positive recollections.

I love to hear older couples share stories of their early dating events. While such rememberings are fun to hear, imagine how much more enjoyable they were to experience. My wife and I are sure to have disappointing episodes and some regretful moments. But one of our goals is to make sure that our positive memories outweigh our heartaches.

𝒟ating Gives You Something to Look Forward To
♥

Cathy and I view our date-nights as sacred. They give each of us something exciting to anticipate. I never grow weary of dating my wife. Actually, when I get depressed about work or tired of the bills or disgusted with the piles of "things to do" around the house, one of the things that best lifts my spirit is the awareness that I'm soon going to be spending special time with Cathy. I eagerly anticipate getting out of the house and being alone with the one person I love more than anyone alive.

We look forward to our dates!

𝒟ating Models Marriage for Your Children
♥

A long-term benefit of dating your spouse is the model you set in place for your children. One of the best ways we can demonstrate love to our children is by expressing affection to our mates. When children have observed their parents placing priority on dating and romance, they will carry that expectation into their own significant relationships.

Kids need to see quality, loving relationships in a world where those aren't the norm. It's not uncommon for kids to fear their parents will get a divorce—half of their friends are children of divorce, and many kids think it's a only a matter of time before it happens to their family. Your dating can relieve a tremendous amount of pressure from your children and set an example they will never forget.

*S*eeing the Big Picture
♥

Two construction workers were busy working on a huge brick-laying project. A passerby was curious about the future of the building. She stopped the workers and asked, "Just what is it you're building?"

The first worker told her he was simply laying bricks trying to finish a construction project. When she asked the second worker the same question he stood and proudly explained to her he was helping to build a great cathedral. He was able to see the big picture, and was excited about the outcome. He viewed his job as a worthy task.

As you think about your own marriage situation you might want to answer that same question, "What are you building?" I hope by the time you finish this book and attempt to apply some of the ideas, you'll be proud to say, "I'm building a great marriage, day by day, year by year, brick by brick!"

Celebrating Marriage

♥

2

*A*s much as I love to watch people, I love to celebrate even more. I can come up with an excuse to celebrate with just about anyone for just about any reason. Like most people, I enjoy the special feeling that comes when we acknowledge someone or something worthy of praise.

Think about the word "celebration" for a moment. What activities come to mind when you focus on that word? What feelings or attitudes do you experience when you celebrate? When was the last time you celebrated? Did your heart fill with joy and enthusiasm? What about celebrating life itself? When was the last time you celebrated your own existence?

Have you ever thrown a party just because you're alive?

*W*e Were Created to
Celebrate Life
♥

I really believe God wants us to celebrate life. I also believe He mourns when we don't applaud the life He's given us, or when we don't live it with meaning and purpose. His love letter to us, the Bible, is quite clear about his purpose for creation. He designed playground Earth with the intention that we should enjoy it.

I know this because of the commitment He made to save the world. He sent Jesus to live and die so we could live forever (John 3:16). Jesus didn't come to steal our joy, kill our dreams, and destroy our lives. He came to give us life worth living. These are *His* words, not mine: "A thief comes to steal, kill, and destroy. I came that you might have life—life in all its fullness" (John 10:10).

*W*e Were Created to
Celebrate Marriage
♥

God is a Father who desires to be in a warm relationship with us. We, too, are social beings who were created to be in relationship with Him and with each other. How do I know this? Because the Bible informs us that God wasn't happy when he created man.

Now He *was* happy when he created the earth. He was thrilled when He brought life to the animals. He was even happy when He designed the plants. God looked at everything he had made and said it was very good. Not okay. Not average. Not even good. But *very* good.

Then God created man and said, "Not good!" Imagine that. Here's Adam, living in the greatest environment—free food, no smog, good health, and even a perfect relationship with God—but it was not good.

Why? Because Adam was incomplete and needed someone to complete him. God had dozens of choices among all the animals to find a suitable companion for Adam. But giraffes, elephants, and rhinos didn't seem to fit the role. Finally God met Adam's need by creating woman and designing the concept of marriage. After creating Eve God said, "So a man will leave his father and mother and be united with his wife. And the two people will become one body" (Genesis 2:24).

Marriage was God's own design, and like the world He made, He also created marriage to be celebrated. What should we celebrate about marriage? We should rejoice in the fact that God loved us enough to give us someone to complete and compliment our lives. If we view God's design the wrong way and view our spouses as competitors instead of as the completion of ourselves, we miss His intent. And this makes it difficult for us to celebrate marriage.

When was the last time you celebrated your marriage? When you think of your marriage, does your heart fill with joy? Are you proud of your spouse?

*M*arriage Is Intended for Pleasure
♥

One question that may come up when you read about God's design for celebrating marriage: "If God had such great intentions, why is marriage such a pain?" I believe marriage is similar to our spirituality, to our walk with the Lord. In both cases, He's given us guidelines to follow because He knows the big picture. Similar to our faith, marriage takes effort and discipline, and sometimes entails pain and struggle. We can't perfect it, but we can work toward moving it in the direction of maturity, just as we do our faith.

Marriage wasn't meant to place restrictions on us, but to provide for us the ultimate in pleasure. This pleasure comes through the support, acceptance, love, and encouragement of our spouse, our "other half."

*G*reat Celebrators Have a Heart for God

♥

Some of the most enjoyable people I know are those who have chosen to celebrate life. The key word in that sentence is "chosen." These individuals have made a conscious effort to make celebration a vital part of their outlook on life. They also have hearts which are directed toward God. I'm not suggesting that people who love life are necessarily the best Christians, or have it all together. But many of them really do love God and want Him to be the center of their lives.

These celebrators of life also understand that God is the source from which love comes. Love doesn't just happen. It isn't something you can buy. And you don't inherit it if you can just wish hard enough. Love is born in one's life through a relationship with God. We read in the Bible, "We should love each other, because love comes from God. The person who loves has become God's child and knows God. Whoever does not love does not know God because God is love" (1 John 4:7,8).

A Love Challenge

♥

It's love—God's love—that makes marriages work and grow. The Scripture that best defines this love is both inspirational and challenging. Allow God's Word to inspire you to action and challenge you to change.

> This love of which I speak is slow to lose patience—it looks for a way of being constructive. It is not possessive: it is neither anxious to impress nor does it cherish inflated ideas of its own importance.
>
> Love has good manners and doesn't pursue selfish advantage. It is not touchy. It does not keep account of evil or gloat over the wickedness of other people. On the contrary, it is glad when truth prevails.
>
> Love knows no limit to its endurance, no end to its trust, no fading of its hope; it can outlast anything. It is, in fact, the one thing that still stands when all else has fallen (1 Corinthians 13:4-7 Phillips).

What a beautiful description of love! To say anything significant about marriage the word love—that kind of love—must be used. I've taken the letters of the word LOVE and developed an acronym to list four important and tangible aspects of this sometimes challenging pursuit.

The "L" stands for *laughter*. Many times laughter can ease a tense moment. Laughter provides great emotional release. It reflects a heart attitude of joy. The Bible defines joy as a happy disposition, reflecting a sense of being right with God as well as with one another. Laughter brings out the enthusiasm that God has placed within each person in His creation.

Use your sense of humor and laughter to enjoy the good times, and to help carry you through some of the difficult times of marriage!

The "O" stands for being *other-centered*. If you want to be successful in your marriage, you're going to have to put your mate's satisfaction ahead of your own. This is tough, especially when you're tired...when you think it's your turn to rest... when you've earned a nap and don't want to take out the trash. Be ready to walk the extra mile, and don't tire of doing special little things for each other. Thinking of ways to put the other person first is a great way to express your love. Be challenged by God's Word, "Love one another...outdo one another in showing honor" (Romans 12:10).

The "V" stands for *value*. How different marriages would be if mates considered one another as being valuable! Your spouse is your gift from God.

Husband, your wife is your queen. Treat her as royalty; cherish her, support her, encourage her— value her.

Wife, treat your husband like a king. Value him and honor him as your prize from God.

Don't wait for the tragedies of others to remind you that your spouse is a treasure. Love each other as Jesus Christ loves His church...unconditionally.

Finally, the "E" stands for *encouragement*. Don't let a day go by without encouraging one another. Learn to make daily deposits into each other's encouragement account. (We'll talk more about this later.)

Wife, let your husband know that you respect him. Encourage him for being romantic. Catch him doing things right in his role as a husband.

Husband, continually look for ways to encourage your wife. Don't let the little things go by unnoticed. Encourage her beauty; her thoughts; her feelings, actions, and opinions. By doing this you will demonstrate your love for her.

Marriage is a challenge, a fulfillment, and a miraculous experience created and ordained by God. Yes, it takes work. But you were created to celebrate your marriage. So let's get the party started!

Keeping Romance in Marriage

♥

3

*I*magine for a moment that you and I are talking through some of the details of your marriage. I have just asked you to describe one of your most vivid romantic moments. Would you have to reach into the archives of your memory for a faded experience that you can hardly remember? Or would you be able to describe, in detail, a romantic time recently shared with the one you love?

Independent of what your answer might be, the mere mention of the word "romance" may stir up a variety of opinions and emotions. Regardless how romance is defined, it almost always brings a sparkle of enthusiasm into the eyes of the one providing the definition. The very mention of the word ignites special feelings and sets the mind wandering.

Romance is difficult to define. It's often depicted through contemporary media with a superficial attractiveness and appeal. But if you look closely at the portrayed context, and examine the motives of the people involved, you'll often find self-centeredness and perversion. Nonetheless, those strong Hollywood images have imprinted upon our imaginations the picture of something nearly everyone feels he or she wants. Unfortunately, this portrait is rarely grounded in reality. And it leaves us more or less confused as we seek an accurate definition. What *is* romance?

𝓜en and Women
Are Different
(In case you didn't know!)
♥

Through a large survey and many conversations about romance, I've learned that most (not all) men view romance in much the same way as it is projected by films, television, and books. When men are asked to define romance they typically use these words: mystery, intrigue, sensuality, lingerie, passion, and never-ending sex.

Woman's definition of romance encompasses a somewhat broader spectrum of qualities. Females describe more practical applications for romance. Examples include talking, anything having to do with being surprised, the husband taking the initiative in getting a baby-sitter or making plans, sincere compliments about physical appearance, short notes of appreciation, gentle touches or physical contact without sexual expectations or motives, and time shared alone.

As I read through the women's surveys I found that less than 5 percent of the women made any reference to sex. However, when my wife read approximately 300 of the women's surveys, she couldn't recall a single one that made direct mention of sex. She accused me of reading sex into 5 percent of the answers! It may be true, because I simply assumed sex would be a natural part of some of the situations the women described.

Cathy explained to me that, for example, falling asleep in one another's arms didn't necessarily mean that the couple made love prior to sleeping. I hadn't thought of it that way.

Our little discussion further demonstrated the fact that many men and women have different definitions and expectations about romance.

Elements of Romance
♥

True romance has to do with simply liking one another. This "liking" is a by-product of a relationship committed to growth. Romance happens as you work together to develop your friendship and attempt to love each other with unconditional acceptance. This type of romance doesn't wear out. Contrary to popular opinion, the magnetism of romance doesn't have to decline as couples age. The good news is that romance is timeless!

I've come up with three elements that I believe contribute significantly to romance: environment, emotion, and enjoyment. Obviously romance can happen without all of these factors, but the combination surely makes for more powerful romantic expressions.

*E*nvironment

Environment is easy to control and manipulate. A well-produced environment can help establish a foundation for emotion. A romantic environment includes various surroundings: music, weather, lighting, ambience, fragrance, visual beauty, and so forth. Of course, this element alone, without at least one of the other two, doesn't produce romance.

*E*motion

The emotion I'm refering to is more passion than fascination. The passion for "wanting" another person is a strong drive. In the survey I mentioned earlier both men and women referred to "being wanted" in their definitions of romance. It's romantic to long for another person, or to be longed for. I believe this yearning draws us toward the satisfaction of our human desire to be needed, cared for, and protected by someone.

One woman wrote, "The most romantic words my husband can say to me are that he hates to travel because he wants to be with me." She felt needed.

A man wrote, "It's easy for me to be passionate about sex, but sex isn't as much fun if my wife doesn't express a similar passion for me. Our best sex is when my wife says she wants me and then treats me accordingly."

*E*njoyment

The enjoyment of one another is by far the most important of the three elements. But sadly, romance can occur without couples enjoying one another. This happens all the time. Two people can be emotional and passionate within the right environment and find themselves deeply entangled in romance. But without really enjoying one another, their romance becomes a shallow and temporary experience.

Enjoyment of one another is the result of hard work and those deposits of encouragement I mentioned in the first two chapters. Enjoyment goes beyond loving each other. It includes liking each other. There's a difference.

A friend's wife recently asked him an interesting question. She said, "Todd, do you like me?"

Todd was a little surprised by the question and said, "Of course I do. I love you."

She then followed his response by saying, "I didn't ask if you loved me. I know you love me. I asked if you liked me."

What she really wanted to know was: Do you enjoy my company? Do you have fun when you are in my presence? Do you like the person I am? Do you enjoy coming home and being with me? She seemed confident of his love but was curious whether he enjoyed her or not.

There are thousands of married couples in our world who have a difficult time being romantic because they don't enjoy each other. They may love one another but they just don't seem to like one another. When you stop liking your mate, passion begins to fizzle. Sometimes this results in a broken marriage. For those couples who don't believe in divorce, the marriage deteriorates until the two are nothing more than roommates who maintain their meaningless titles "Mr. and Mrs."

Enjoying each other makes it possible for you and your mate to be friends. And it's in this healthy soil that emotion grows into a romantic, rewarding relationship.

Romancing
Creatively

♥

4

*A*dding creativity to your dating and romantic experiences will add sparkle to your time together. It will also communicate a message to your spouse that he or she is worth the time and energy required to bring about a great memory. You and your mate will never forget a creative date.

One of the major roadblocks to creativity is the statement, "I don't have a creative bone in my body." Some men and women assume that creativity is a gift for a select few. The truth is, everyone has the potential to think and be creative. Originality is found within individuals and can't be purchased from institutions. You *can* be creative. You may need a little

41

push, a dose of assurance, or a few exercises to get you going. But you can do it!

Another roadblock appears when people talk about the creativity of others and feel inadequate because they don't seem to match up. They might say, "You should meet Scott. Now there's a creative person!" Or, "Mary is always doing creative things for her husband—things I could never think of!" This type of thinking typically leads to discouragement. When you compare your skills with others', you usually end up disappointed. A principle of living should be to better yourself and not to compare or compete with others. Don't count yourself out just because you think someone else is more creative than you are.

The goal of this chapter is to show you how easily you can become more imaginative by introducing five simple steps. If you don't believe you're very original, these five ideas may appear overwhelming. On the other hand, if you are currently using your creative juices this chapter may appear elementary. Either way, please read on, and think of ways in which you can personalize each action.

Start with Variety
♥

One of the simplest forms of creativity is variety. Anyone who has the ability to make choices can apply variety to dating and romantic situations. Begin with a normal situation and spice up your time with variations.

Let's use a dinner-date as an example:

♥ | If you always eat at the same restaurant switch to a new one.

♥ | Walk instead of drive.

- ♥ Sit on the same side of the booth instead of across from one another.

- ♥ Order different kinds of food.

- ♥ Break your after-dinner routine and go sightseeing.

- ♥ When you return, enter the house through the backyard instead of the front door.

- ♥ Don't check your answering machine.

- ♥ Go straight to the fireplace and start a fire instead of going to bed.

- ♥ Relax and talk about your old dating days before you were married.

Brainstorm Ideas
♥

My best ideas come when I intentionally stretch my brain a little. And during brainstorming sessions with myself, my friends, or a management team I abide by one rule: No idea is a bad idea. This rule allows freedom for the mind to wander and not be inhibited by fear of embarrassment. It's often some of the wackiest mental tangents that trigger the best ideas.

When I want to put together a creative date for my wife I begin with a blank sheet of paper.

- ♥ On one side of the paper I'll write a brief sentence describing my goal (how I hope Cathy feels during our time together) for the evening.

♥ | Then I list various segments of the date (location, transportation, etc.) and begin to brainstorm different options for each segment.

♥ | Once I've exhausted my options I usually have several choices to choose from.

*H*onor Individuality
♥

Respect for individuality is more a principle in caring for your spouse than it is an exercise in creativity. Nonetheless, it's an essential aspect of the creative process.

You know that every person is different. And chances are good that you know just exactly how different your spouse is from you! Actually, those differences may have been the qualities that initially attracted you to your mate. Now those same differences may be driving you crazy. It's so easy to consciously or subconsciously try to mold our spouses into our own images instead of trying to complement our differences, recognizing their uniqueness.

Sense the individuality of the other person and try to honor it by creatively choosing ideas, situations, and environments that are favorable to your mate's personality. If you want him or her to have the best time possible, design a date suited for your mate's individual personality. I'm not suggesting that you never try ideas outside of your spouse's comfort zone. But if you're too experimental, I'm afraid your future creative attempts won't be viewed with much delight or anticipation.

Become a Listener
♥

I almost hate to put this in print because I don't want her to know, but my greatest creative secret is that I'm a great listener to my wife. I listen to the likes and desires that she communicates through everyday conversation.

For example, recently we were talking about a baby shower she attended. As she described the event, I heard her make a positive comment about her friend Linda's outfit and how cute it was. She probably told me 20 things about the day, but I noticed her face became a little more animated when she described Linda's outfit. I heard the excitement in her voice. Her intention wasn't to motivate me to go out and buy her a new outfit, but that's exactly what I did. I called Linda, found out the details, and had a perfect gift for my wife.

You'll see an example on the next page of some details you might want to listen for and note. I keep this sheet away from my wife's view but continually add to it as I hear new comments. By doing this I'm assured that my creative attempts will fulfill Cathy's desires and act as a surprise at the same time.

Copy and Adapt
♥

Many years ago I heard someone say, "The essence of creativity is to copy the ideas of other people." I love that concept! I copied the quote and adjusted it to read like this, "The essence of creativity is based on your ability to copy and adapt to your personal situation."

The adaptation to your personal situation and your mate's individuality becomes crucial if you want to

Favorite colors:
Favorite type of music:
Favorite travel destinations:
Favorite foods:
Favorite desserts:
Surprise ideas:
Favorite influential people:
Favorite hobbies:
Favorite flowers:
He/she hates:
Favorite sports/pastimes:
Favorite fantasies:
Pet peeves:
Favorite personality likes/dislikes:
Other special interests:
Favorite toothpaste:
Things that are embarrassing to him/her:
Favorite perfume/cologne:
Best friends:
Favorite books:
Favorite cartoon character:
Dream car:
Favorite movies:
Favorite gift ideas:
Clothing styles:
Clothing sizes:
Favorite animals:
Favorite drinks:
Favorite retreat spots:
Where he/she parks:
Favorite restaurants:
Work schedule:

please your spouse. As a matter of fact, I sincerely hope that you will read the ideas in this book and adapt "pieces" of them in order to fit your personal situation.

Ezekiel said it best when he made the statement, "There's nothing new under the sun." If this is true, find ideas that have worked elsewhere and tweak them to fit your individual circumstances. Allow the creative victories of others to cut down on your planning time.

I'm aware that many people reading this book resist change. Habits can become like an old pair of shoes—so comfortable you can't get rid of them. Adding creativity to your romantic situations and dating experiences will force you to change. But the change will be rewarded.

Please understand that I'm not suggesting you be creative every moment of your life. However, I do believe that you can be more creative than you are right now. Try taking these five "baby steps" towards creativity. They will provide you with a scrapbook of happy memories!

Elements of a Romantic Date

♥

5

*T*his chapter is designed to give you an easy-to-remember format for creating your own romantic dates. Keep in mind that each dating experience should be unique, formed with differing variables to make the experience memorable. Rather than providing a checklist of "20 things you should do" to ensure creative and romantic dates, I've provided seven elements that should always be considered during date planning. These elements are:

Fun
Attitude
Newness
Time
Attention
Surprise
Yes!

There is no absolute prescribed order, but the first letter of each element forms a memorable acronym: FANTASY. Now this word isn't intended to promote erotic thoughts, but instead to depict a fairy-tale image of love, romance, and a happy ending.

Naturally each date doesn't need to contain all these elements to be successful. And if you're not presently dating your spouse at all, any one of these elements is better than none. You will find, though, that a combination of them promises a far more memorable time.

I know for a fact that these principles work. And when they are gently applied with your personal, individual touch, they will have a powerful impact on your time together and will enhance the strengthening of your marriage.

Let your F.A.N.T.A.S.Y. begin!

F = FUN
♥

Fun is a perfect word for recounting an enjoyable event. When a date is described as "fun," an overall, pleasant time is implied. A description of the date is usually accompanied by both verbal and nonverbal excitement, which illustrates that "a good time was had by all!"

As I read the book of Genesis, I can't help but believe we were created to enjoy life and one another. I think God wants us to have fun in the course of our lives, and I'm convinced that marriages would be far stronger if they were more playful.

When I conduct premarital counseling, the most common reason couples give for getting married is that they want to continue for a lifetime enjoying the fun they share now. Unfortunately, I rarely hear this comment from married couples describing their on-going relationships. In spite of this, and contrary to some rumors, marriage can be fun.

I don't want to give the impression that dates must be creative in order to be fun. Recently Cathy and I went bowling—I wouldn't qualify this as a creative date, but nonetheless we had a great time. There was plenty to laugh about: the ugly rental shoes, my slipping on the oiled lane and falling on my back, Cathy rolling five gutterballs in a row. Furthermore, neither one of us knew how to keep score.

But we did have fun!

One of the greatest challenges we all face is learning to have fun without any external aid. If you can "create" fun from nothing you'll be at an advantage. Even the greatest "toys" on earth will eventually become boring if you don't know how to have fun without them.

𝓐 = Attitude
♥

In my experience with people, I've found that the most enjoyable individuals to be around are those with positive attitudes about life. Attitudes precede actions. In my endeavors to treat Cathy like a queen I must maintain a loving and romantic attitude. When I fall short in making her feel special, it can usually be traced back to a negative or inconsistent attitude.

An important element in discovering the intimacy in a relationship is refocusing our attitudes. I'm not suggesting you enroll in a PMA (positive mental attitude) class or spend hours reading self-help books. But I am suggesting you keep a romantic attitude toward your spouse in the forefront of your mind. Chances are, positive romantic actions will follow.

It's difficult for a romantic experience or a creative date to fail when your actions spring forth from an attitude that wants the best for your husband or wife.

𝒩 = New
♥

The introduction of something new can help create both romance and creativity. Newness might be reflected in such things as dress, location, timing, mood, and spirit.

Newness also interrelates with most of the other elements. For example, doing just about anything new has higher potential for fun than doing something you've done a thousand times before. Newness reflects a fresh and exciting attitude.

There are a few things to remember. First of all, attempting a new diversion may take a bit of extra time. And there may be risks involved. But it is a worthwhile effort, because surprise and delight are typically the accompaniment of new things.

Best of all, any new effort communicates the "yes!" message—the message you want to give, as well as the one you want to receive.

7 = Time
♥

If you attempt to incorporate any or all of these elements, the process will take a fair portion of your time. You'll find your most creative and romantic dates require preparation. It's not easy to design a successful creative date on the spur of the moment.

Taking time is romantic. My wife loves it when I spend time on something directed toward her or strengthening our relationship. Even if our date is a bomb, she's thrilled that I was willing to take the time, trying to make something wonderful happen.

"No time" is one of the major excuses I hear from couples who don't date. Unfortunately, some couples give more time to cleaning their garages than to communicating and caring for one another. In my opinion, this lack of quality time is one of the major contributors to the breakdown of the American family.

Time is precious. Time is easily wasted. And time is needed to develop a creative and romantic date, as well as a successful marriage.

𝒜 = Attention
♥

Giving your spouse attention is a simple concept, but one that's indispensable to the success of quality time together. By answering the following four questions you will be able to determine whether you're winning at this one.

♥ | Do you really pay attention to your spouse?
♥ | When you are together are you "all there"?
♥ | Do you communicate with your eyes?
♥ | Does your spouse feel like he or she is the center or the object of your attention?

Before your date, insert the word "attention" into your attitude vocabulary. Make sure your spouse feels he or she got your full focus and consideration.

S = Surprise

♥

I believe surprise is the most difficult element to be incorporated into dating, but the rewards are often the most satisfying. During the unfolding of a surprise you will see some of your spouse's most sincere feelings, because the element of surprise usually ignites an emotional response.

I love to surprise my wife on our dates, and therefore I spend the majority of my planning time dreaming up ways to do so. In its simplest form, surprise may include keeping your dating location a mystery. A more complex form of surprise might take place when a friend dresses up like a medieval knight and delivers a gift to your shocked wife in the middle of a crowded restaurant.

Y = Yes!
The Yes! Message

♥

The response of the receiver is as vital to the dating or romantic experience as the idea itself. When energy has been put into developing a creative, romantic experience, there is usually a feeling of fear associated with the attempt—the fear of failing, the fear of looking or acting stupid or the fear of doing something that didn't meet the needs of your spouse. These fears are calmed when he or she communicates a sense of approval. This approval is what I call the yes! message.

Receiving the yes! message gives hope, and encourages future attempts. When your spouse goes out on a limb to try something new, creative, or romantic, you can send an encouraging message by affirming the attempt.

Remember to think of the word FANTASY when you plan your next special date with your spouse. By incorporating each of the ideas in the acronym, you'll find that your dating life is enriched, and that your marriage is filled with new and exciting opportunities and memories.

200
Romantic Things
You Could Easily Do
(But Probably Aren't Doing!)

♥

6

*B*efore you begin reading this chapter, I feel compelled to offer a few warnings, statements, and principles that I hope will help you appreciate and understand the method behind my madness!

A) A few of these ideas may be too outrageous for your style. That's okay. Read the idea, shake your head in wonder, and mutter, "Some people are really bizarre." I developed this list with the hope that each couple would add to or subtract from it in order to meet their individual needs. You may find the outrageous ideas are helpful in stretching your imagination and pushing you toward becoming more creative.

B) You may also come across some ideas that appear rather ordinary or humdrum. An example of this would be holding hands. I, too, once thought hand-holding was a simplistic idea, but my own personal surveys have shown me otherwise. Start by mastering the basics.

C) There are other ideas that may appear more thoughtful than romantic. These ideas become romantic when they are accomplished with the right attitude and caring emotions. They will be received with a thankful response.

D) I don't want to be guilty of sounding sexist! You can be sure that my ideas about "creative ro-romance" can be applied both to husbands and wives. I may use the words "him" or "her," but either spouse can dedicate the majority of these ideas to the other.

E) I hope you realize the importance of encouraging your spouse's efforts. Even if you don't see the romantic gesture you've been dreaming about, even if the timing isn't perfect, express your appreciation warmly. There are few things that make us feel worse than being rejected after we've made an effort to please.

F) Give some thought to how your spouse might react to these ideas before trying them. Your spouse's state of mind and personality will help you determine whether the attempt is appropriate for your marriage, or even worth the effort. Whatever you do, be sensitive!

G) Don't allow your age to be the excuse keeping you from trying a few new ideas. I have a 72-year-old friend who tells me, "We are only as old as our attitudes allow us to be." So whether you're 20 or 80, make an effort to experiment with some of these concepts and see what happens to your marriage.

Now—for the 200 ideas! Here they are:

1. Sketch your dream-house floor plan and talk about the possibilities for each room.
2. Take a bath together.
3. Write the love story of how you met. Get it printed and bound.
4. List your spouse's best qualities in alphabetical order.
5. Tour a museum or an art gallery.
6. Park in a secluded area and kiss in your car.
7. Make your own movie scene—stop and kiss on a bridge as the sun is setting.
8. Place great emphasis on the little changes she makes concerning her appearance.
9. Give your wife a bath and wash her hair.
10. Float on a raft together.
11. Take a stroll around the block.
12. Pick your wife up and carry her away from the kitchen while she is cooking. Sauté her with kisses.
13. Stock the cupboards with food she loves to eat but usually won't buy for herself. (Don't do this if she's dieting!)
14. Give him a back rub.
15. Rent a classic love-story video and watch it while cuddling under blankets.
16. Give your spouse a body massage.
17. Walk through model homes and dream about your next house. Steal a kiss in a closet.
18. Stroll around a nearby lake.
19. Sit in front of the fireplace and talk.
20. Read to one another in bed.
21. Take a horse-drawn carriage ride.

22. Turn the lights down during dinner.
23. Make a surprise long distance call to your spouse while you're out of town (in addition to your scheduled calls).
24. Play music in your bedroom.
25. Go swimming in the middle of the night.
26. Shave your wife's legs.
27. Shave your husband's face.
28. Write a poem for your spouse.
29. Run through the sprinklers on a hot day.
30. Remember to look into your spouse's eyes while she tells you about her day.
31. Make up nicknames for each other.
32. Go the extra mile to please your mate.
33. When you are the one who is correct during a discussion, give your spouse a kiss. Focus on your love rather than who is right.
34. Tell your spouse, "I'm glad I married you!"
35. Fulfill one of your spouse's fantasies.
36. Hug your husband from behind and give him a kiss on the back of the neck.
37. Stop in the middle of your busy day and talk to your spouse for 15 minutes.
38. Create your own special holiday.
39. In case you've forgotten, place your hand on your spouse's leg when you're riding in the car.
40. Send your wife a compliment through one of her friends or colleagues.
41. Ask for an isolated booth in a restaurant.
42. Become your spouse's cheerleader when she's had a terrible day.
43. Tell your wife, "I love you because..." (You'll have to finish the sentence. I can't be responsible for everything!)
44. Show your wife affection while she is talking to one of her friends.
45. Sleep in a sleeping bag together.

46. Do something your spouse loves to do, even though it doesn't interest you personally.
47. Go horseback riding on the same horse.
48. Photocopy a newspaper cartoon and write your own romantic caption.
49. Photocopy romantic words from the dictionary and leave them in places your spouse will find them.
50. Cut out romantic photos from magazines and write your own encouraging messages on them.
51. While driving, pull over for scenic sights and get out of the car to take in the panoramic beauty.
52. Write your spouse affirming love letters.
53. Mail your spouse love letters instead of leaving them in the house.
54. Feed ducks together (you can feed any type of animal as long as it's not a housepet—the idea is to get outside together).
55. Build a snowman together.
56. Watch the sun come up or go down.
57. Go fishing together with only one pole.
58. Sit on the same side of a restaurant booth.
59. Spontaneously spend the entire day together away from the house.
60. Picnic by a pond.
61. Give your mate a foot massage.
62. Put on perfume or after-shave before going out.
63. Go skinny-dipping.
64. Develop a code word for sex that you can use when you're a part of a crowd.
65. Buy your husband or wife a new outfit.
66. Sing a song to your spouse.
67. Let go of helium balloons and watch them race each other out of sight.
68. Buy her a stuffed animal.
69. Write "I love you" in the dust around the house instead of complaining about it.

70. Set up a surprise manicure, hair styling, or mud-bath appointment for your spouse.
71. Put together a puzzle on a rainy night.
72. Read a romance novel together.
73. Rent a boat.
74. Take a train ride.
75. Ride bikes in the rain.
76. Read poetry to one another.
77. Build sand castles on the beach.
78. Take a moonlight canoe ride.
79. Make your spouse a greeting card.
80. Swing together on a playground.
81. Go for a midnight dip in a hot tub.
82. Give your wife a balloon bouquet.
83. Take a bath in Jell-O.
84. Make heart-shaped pancakes and serve them in bed.
85. Surprise your husband by ordering for him the next time you go to a restaurant (make sure he likes what you order).
86. Dress up and deliver a singing telegram.
87. Take a hot-air balloon ride.
88. Walk through a housing construction site and kiss in each of the houses.
89. Count the stars.
90. Go on a gondola ride.
91. Bring a late-night snack or drink to bed.
92. Tell your spouse, "I'd rather be with you right here than any place in the world."
93. Whisper something romantic to your spouse in a crowded room.
94. Have a candlelight picnic in the backyard.
95. Play tennis at night under a full moon using no lights.
96. Develop a weekly dining spot to meet for lunch.
97. Share a long piece of licorice without using your hands.

98. Make cookies by candlelight.
99. Unscrew the table light-bulb at your restaurant booth to dim the lights.
100. Put perfume on your bed sheets.
101. Leave encouraging notes for your spouse that he will find at different times throughout the week.
102. Put on old clothes and go play in the mud, and then shower together.
103. Hold hands while roller skating.
104. Write out 50 reasons you're glad to be married.
105. Tickle-wrestle in bed.
106. Go on a walk and pick flowers.
107. Put an "I love you!" message in her lunch.
108. Place a rose on her pillow.
109. Set candles above the bed (carefully!).
110. Serve breakfast in bed.
111. Hide small gifts that your spouse will find throughout the week.
112. Sit and listen carefully to one another.
113. Tuck your wife into bed, read her a goodnight story and kiss her on the forehead.
114. Remember how you used to laugh at his silly jokes or things he thought were funny? Do it again.
115. Write a song for your spouse.
116. Go for a walk barefoot.
117. Sit in a pond where the water goes up to your waist.
118. Splash each other.
119. Spend an entire day in the middle of nowhere (when you find it, let me know where it is).
120. Dance in your candlelit living room.
121. Walk on the beach.
122. Play a board game by the fire.
123. Reminisce through old photo albums.
124. Go away for the weekend.

125. Go for a moonlit walk down a street of beautiful homes.
126. Rub feet under the table.
127. Kiss in a crowded area.
128. Sit on his lap even when there's sitting room elsewhere.
129. Drink from the same glass.
130. Kiss in the rain.
131. Join him, unexpectedly, in the shower.
132. Wear his boxer shorts and...well, that's all.
133. Whisper to your spouse how sexy she is.
134. Buy your husband a negligee that you know you'll look great in.
135. Brush her hair.
136. Ride a carousel or a merry-go-round.
137. Take a bike ride—on the same bike.
138. Hug as you roll down a hill (if you ever want to do this again you'd better choose a grassy hill).
139. Play doctor.
140. Read off of one menu.
141. Share a milk shake with two straws.
142. Take the phone off the hook, turn off the TV, turn down the lights and kiss on the floor.
143. Put fresh flowers in front of her bathroom sink and write a love note with lipstick on the mirror.
144. Dedicate a song to her over the radio.
145. Break away from the chaos of the family long enough to share an intimate conversation.
146. Wink and smile at your spouse from across the room.
147. Kiss your spouse's fingers.
148. Celebrate for no reason.
149. Leave a photo of yourself on his dashboard.
150. Give your husband a manicure.
151. Before entering a restaurant tell your husband you're not wearing any underwear.
152. Fill your bed with rose petals.

153. Send your kids to the babysitter and then play hide-and-seek.
154. Remember something she thinks you've forgotten.
155. Stand together in front of a lake and watch your reflections.
156. Sunbathe in an isolated location.
157. Hug for an extended period of time.
158. Leave your lip-prints on a love note.
159. Sit in front of the window during a rainstorm.
160. Bake cookies together.
161. Do something to help.
162. Take a fun class together.
163. Go rock-skipping.
164. Ride a bicycle-built-for-two.
165. Fall asleep holding each other.
166. Draw your spouse a stick-figure picture of something romantic.
167. Tell your spouse you will take her anywhere she wants to go.
168. Call your spouse during the day and remind him of your love for him.
169. Pour the cream in his coffee for him.
170. Decide not to go to a social event at the last minute and instead go somewhere alone.
171. Have a hot bubble bath ready for her when she comes home from a long day.
172. Wear a negligee around the house (if you're a female!).
173. Read a book about sex or romantic massage.
174. Ask your spouse, "What can I do to make you happier?"
175. Order a catalog of sexy bed-clothes.
176. Make love in a new place.
177. Ask for the honeymoon suite when you go to a hotel.
178. Buy new satin sheets.

179. Tell him what turns you on.
180. Leave teasing notes around the house to create an atmosphere of anticipation.
181. Use a tender-touch as you pass one another around the house.
182. Commit yourself to removing a "hang-up" that keeps you from being romantic.
183. Reminisce about your first kiss or your first date.
184. Plant a tree together in honor of your marriage.
185. Find the words to express your passion for your spouse.
186. Go kite flying.
187. Read a loving passage about your spouse from your journal.
188. Hold hands.
189. Go up on the roof to watch the sunset.
190. Bring home flowers.
191. Undress in front of your husband.
192. Tell your spouse what you see when you look into her eyes.
193. Dress your best and go somewhere special.
194. Play a new sport together.
195. Attend a sporting event you've never been to together.
196. Surprise your spouse with an ice-cold drink while he or she is working hard on a hot day.
197. Fill the freezer with her favorite desserts.
198. Mail a love letter to your spouse's place of work.
199. Take time to think about him during the day, then tell him what you thought.
200. Drop everything and do something for the one you love—right now!

Play
with a Purpose

♥

7

"Play" within the context of marriage has a far broader meaning than sex. This chapter has nothing to do with sex, but has a great deal to do with intimacy. Play is an exciting form of communication and expression.

We encourage children to play because we view it as a healthy factor in their development. Psychologists have even gone so far as to study child's play and to formulate philosophical theories based on hours of observation. But as children grow older we adults tend to discourage their play and instruct them to "grow up!" Finally, when they reach their adult years, their ability to play receives little respect and is often described as immaturity. Because of this, most adults view play as childish.

There is something very pure and beautiful about play. I'd like to believe that when Jesus said, "The kingdom of heaven belongs to people who are like these children," He was referring, at least in part, to their ability to enjoy life through play. Adults take pride in maturity, and yet the words of Jesus seem to affirm a certain expression of immaturity.

As adults, I'm not sure we can be taught how to play, since playfulness is more of an attitude than a learned skill. I do believe, however, that we can learn to create an atmosphere where play comes naturally to us, and we can seize opportunities which seem conducive to play.

I don't have an articulate definition which fully encompasses what I mean by "play." But the following seven words bring clarity to what I'm trying to say. As you read my definition, I hope you will give play your own meaning and apply this unique form of communication to your own marriage. I can promise that it will naturally evolve as you and your spouse begin to interact with humor and delight.

Laughter: One of the true highlights in my marriage is making my wife laugh. It may sound simple, but I love doing it. Laughter is one of the common denominators within healthy families, and I want my home environment to include laughter that is both natural and familiar.

Do you and your spouse share laughter on a regular basis? I'm not referring to chuckling over the newest television sitcom. I'm suggesting the laughter that comes from the heart and communicates internal joy and happiness. This type of laughter is healthy and necessary. And an incident of uncontrollable giggling usually creates a lifetime memory. I'd even go so far as to say that there may be something ailing in your relationship if laughter isn't a frequent occurrence.

Adventure: Adding adventure to your marriage will cause you to move out of your comfort zones and to experience life from new angles. Recently, Cathy and I drove to the top of a hill to look at the midnight city lights (well, to be honest, we were going to neck in the car). At the top of the hill was a beautiful college campus. We decided to go on an adventure and explore the campus with the moonlight as our guide.

Cathy and I felt as if we were being really sneaky when we ended up in the dugout at the school's baseball field. We found ourselves sitting on the benches talking, giggling and kissing—all under the illusion that we were alone. Suddenly a maintenance worker flashed a light on us and chased us away! We were a little embarrassed about getting caught. But the adventure was one we'll never forget.

Acting silly: I believe the freedom to act silly in front of our spouses is a simple yet important joy of life. By being silly, I'm referring to things like singing off key without fear of embarrassment, talking in a strange voice just to be stupid, and putting your arm around a store's mannequin with the hope of bringing a smile to a stranger.

Many professions keep people from expressing themselves freely. And an outlet of silliness can become a source of release, allowing the child inside us to come out and play.

Bed talk: When I speak to women's groups, the wives who attend always want ideas about how they should initiate talk with their husbands. Finding a way to share intimate conversation seems to be one of their greatest needs.

Women find it very special to lie in bed with the lights out, just to talk, giggle, tickle, and be together. This time becomes a highlight of their day, especially meaningful when it's done without the expectation of their time ending with sex.

Practical jokes: Constructive pranks which are more amusing than harmful have a great way of creating a playful atmosphere for some couples. Bear in mind that some people don't respond well to this sort of thing, and husbands and wives need to be sensitive both to the personality and state of mind of their mates.

In our home, the practical jokes began some time ago, when I turned off the bathroom light while Cathy was showering. She retaliated by taking all the towels and clothes from the bathroom the next time I was in the shower.

The next day I responded by throwing a bucket of cold water on her while she showered. Weeks later I found my underwear in the freezer. I reciprocated by filling her medicine cabinet with marbles, which she discovered in the middle of the night while searching for cold medicine. She countered by filling my briefcase with marshmallows. The jokes continue. And we both relish the laughter shared when the other person experiences a love-prank.

Imagination: I love to imagine and dream. I also enjoy hearing my wife share her dreams. Sometimes we take the time to ask each other questions that stretch our imaginations. We might be driving in the car, sitting in a restaurant, or lying around the house. Cathy will ask me an imaginative question. For example, "If you could live anywhere in the world where would you want to live?"

Answers to imaginary questions give us greater insight into each other, and allow us to roam about in a fantasy world for a little while. Here are a few examples to get you going:

- ♥ If you could have your choice between being rich or famous which would you choose?

- ♥ If you could spend a day with anyone famous, who would it be and what would you want to do?

- ♥ What would you do if you only had one week to live?

- ♥ If someone gave you $1,000,000 and you couldn't spend the money on yourself or your family, who would you give it to?

Spontaneity: It's difficult to be spontaneous when we live in a structured world that forces us to live by our calendars. Worse yet, I'm one of those people who tends to plan even my unplanned time. Every once in a while I'll break loose and do something impulsive, and it usually produces a great time of fun. An attitude of spontaneity breeds a positive attitude of play.

Plan to get up some morning and head out in the car with the absolute determination that you aren't going to plan one single thing. (No fair secretly heading for your favorite restaurant at lunch time, either!) Just drive north, south, east, or west, and stop when you feel like it. Look in a shop or at a garage sale, take a picture, or go for a walk on a pier. Go wherever you feel like going, discover new territory, and explore unknown spots. If possible, inform the baby-sitter that you're not sure when you'll be home.

Things like laughter, adventure, acting silly, and using your imagination help define "play" for us grownups. My explanations, and for that matter, my suggestions, may not fit into your style or your vocabulary. However, if you are open to change and daring enough to venture into "playing together," I'm confident you'll be rewarded in your marriage.

True play is nothing more than a childlike way of celebrating life. Remember, "The kingdom of heaven belongs to people who become like these children."

14
Creative Date
Strategies

♥

8

Lottery Month

♥

Study your monthly calendar and choose at least two days on which you can schedule something special for your mate. Mark those days on your calendar as a reminder, but keep them to yourself, as a surprise. When one of the days arrives, go out of your way to do something special to communicate your love. If your spouse asks, "Why did you do this?" or "What was this for?" tell him (or her) it's because you love him—nothing more needs to be said.

We all need reminders—thoughtfulness is easy to forget. And each of us needs special occasions we can look forward to.

This idea will help keep you on the romantic track.

*A*bsentee Arrangement
♥

If you are going to be away from home for a significant amount of time, there are many things you can do to keep yourself in the picture during your absence. One easy way is to leave notes, cards, tape-recorded messages, flowers, and other personalized gifts around the house in places where they are sure to be discovered. You can also ask friends to help you deliver surprises every day you are absent.

These romantic gestures remind your mate that you are thinking of her. You'll also find that a series of special surprises will decrease the distance between you two.

*Y*ellow Pages Scavenger Hunt
♥

Let your spouse's fingers do the walking as you take her on a hunt she will never forget. Advertisers claim everything can be found in the Yellow Pages. If this is true you will have hundreds of ideas to choose from to put together an exciting date.

Here's an example of how your Yellow Pages can help with a creative date:

Leave a note on top of the Yellow Pages instructing your spouse to turn to page 263.

When she finds page 263 she will notice that you highlighted the ad for Bob's Florist Shop and scribbled a note telling her to look in the bathtub.

When she checks the bathtub she finds a rose accompanied by a note with the words "Retail—page 598."

When she looks up page 598 in the Yellow Pages she will find Betty's Cards and Gifts highlighted with a personalized footnote instructing her to check the junk drawer in the closet.

When she searches the closet drawer she will find a card from you. Inside the card is a torn-out yellow page with the heading "Restaurant."

When she finds the highlighted restaurant there's a scribbled note reading, "Dinner at 7:00."

This idea can be continued as long as you can keep your spouse's attention! I'm confident you'll keep her occupied as she lets her fingers do the walking to keep up with your creativity.

*G*uinness Book Date
♥

By attempting to break a record in the *Guinness Book of World Records* you will not only have a great time but you have the potential of becoming famous! Pick up a copy of the book's latest edition and search through the contents until you come across an idea that you two may have a shot at. If you don't find any that are worth trying you are guaranteed to have great conversation, wondering why some people would try such crazy things. Here are a couple of ideas to get you started:

♥ Put together the largest jig-saw puzzle (15,520 pieces).

♥ Do the hula-hoop for the longest amount of time (88 hours).

♥ Try to quickly eat 100 yards of spaghetti (12.02 seconds).

♥ Break the record for longest pushing of a baby carriage (345 miles in 24 hours).

♥ Dance till you break the ballroom dancing record (120 hours).

*7*raveling Photographer
♥

Some people find it natural to use a camera for birthdays, anniversaries, and weekend dates. Others consider a camera to be a foreign object. Either way, I'm suggesting you begin by bringing a small camera whenever you go on a date. In doing so, you'll find it easy to maintain and document great moments to remember.

Regardless of the date's significance, force yourself to take pictures as often as you can. Photos make great presents, especially if they're put in small frames or combined in a scrapbook. If you take this idea seriously, your photos will soon become some of your most prized possessions.

*S*pecial Spots
♥

Try designating different locations where you've had great experiences as your personal "special spots." The place may be a tree-swing, or the cliff where you saw a beautiful sunset, or the hills near the deserted cabin where you went for a walk, or the French restaurant across town. No matter where your best memories happened, once those places are labeled as "special spots," your presence there will have far deeper meaning. A simple walk through your special park will become an incredible gesture of love. And an ordinary dinner on a Wednesday night will turn into a romantic evening—all because of the location, and what it means to you.

*O*utfit to Go
♥

Most people enjoy buying a new outfit for a special date. Next time you feel the urge to splurge, do it with your spouse—buy yourselves new clothes. Allow a couple of extra hours before your planned date, and drive to a mall dressed in your grubbies. Browse the clothing shops and discuss the style of dress you want for your date (dressy, casual, elegant, etc.). Try things on for each other, buy what you like, and enjoy your evening in style.

*G*et Lost
♥

Next time you attend a large event drop your wife off near its entrance before parking the car. After the event is over, pretend you've forgotten where you've parked. Be relaxed and slowly stroll through the parking lot cuddled with your wife. Inform her about the positive aspect of misplacing the car—which is giving the two of you time alone, outside, to enjoy one another. This is a much better use of time than sitting in the car waiting for the traffic to exit the parking lot anyway.

If you're married to the type of person who is going to call you an "idiot" for misplacing the car, you may want to skip this idea.

*M*inidate
♥

There will be times when so much is going on within your family that you can't possibly find the time to date. When you know it's going to be a hectic week, you can still set aside 30 minutes to be together, even amidst the busyness.

Get outside the house and invest a few minutes of time in one another. Granted, this may not be as rewarding as a regular date, but it's much better than not doing anything at all. Furthermore, if you initiate the desire to spend time during a busy time you will score "big points" in the thoughtful-category. If his assumption was that you wouldn't have even a second together, you'll surpass his expectations by squeezing in a few minutes.

*H*otel Surprise
♥

Reserve a room for one night at a local hotel without your spouse's knowledge. Tell him you would like to go to dinner at the hotel's restaurant. Check in and get the key without letting him know. After eating, walk around and browse through the lobby and shops, and find the swimming pool and jacuzzi. Before leaving, suggest a romantic ride in the elevator. When the elevator stops at your floor, surprise him by escorting him to your "love suite" for a one-night slumber party.

With a little research you may find some of the nicer hotels have discount rates on Friday and Saturday nights. And, by the way, be sure the family budget can afford this little romantic adventure before you make the reservations!

*G*ood Ol' Days
♥

If you can remember the details of your first date you'll have a great time trying to recreate as much of it as you can. If your first date was a positive experience you'll spend time reminiscing over feelings and thoughts that accompanied your time together.

If your first date was a failure, forget this idea. Instead, spend the time giving thanks that you ever made it to a second date!

*T*wenty-Dollar Weekend
♥

You'll have to provide the locations but here's the idea: Try to go away for the weekend and spend only $20. You'll have to be more than creative, you'll have to be frugal. You may need to go camping or stay at a friend's "getaway." Sleeping in the car will mean that you probably won't get far from home. But you'll have a fun time trying to be creative, meeting all your needs, and keeping yourselves under budget.

*P*in the Tail on the Date Board
♥

Attach a city or area map to a wall and highlight all the different areas that would be realistic for a date (restaurants, activities, scenic walks, etc.). Blindfold your spouse and explain that this game is similar to

Pin the Tail on the Donkey. After spinning her around a few times have her walk to the map and stick a pin into a section of the map. Then take her to the spots closest to where she placed the pin.

*M*y Time Is Yours
♥

In the midst of busy schedules, deadlines, and pressures, there are days when our time with our spouses is limited. Here's an idea to spend your time the way your mate would most enjoy.

Make a chart similar to the one below and give him or her the option of how your time together would best be spent.

♥ My Time Is Yours ♥

I wish I could spend all day with you but today it looks like we'll only have _____ minutes/hours together. Since I want to do whatever you want to do, please write an amount of time next to the activity you would most like to do. I'll take the responsibility of seeing that we stay on schedule.

Activity   **# of Minutes**

Talking
Hugging
Reading
Making love
Walking
Eating
Listening to music
Playing games
Praying
Driving around
Playing with the kids
Cleaning house
Shopping
Other: _____

Romance at Home

♥

9

There are dozens of reasons for saying "Let's stay home!" Some people struggle with tight budgets, a lack of transportation, unreliable baby-sitters and, occasionally, bad weather. I'm convinced that you and your spouse can still enjoy each other's company, both creatively and romantically, even when you decide not to leave the house. You'll find this chapter has several options for Home Dates. By the way, these aren't to be used as cop-outs for people who hate to leave their recliners. They are, instead, creative alternatives. With a little energy invested, you may find yourselves having the time of your lives. After all, home is where the heart is.

Dinner Room Theater
♥

Transform your home into an exciting house of entertainment by giving each room a unique purpose. For example, decorate your dining room as a elegant restaurant and begin your evening sharing a gourmet meal.

After dinner, move to the living room which is prepared to deliver a classical concert the instant you turn on the stereo.

Once you've satisfied your more serious musical tastes, move to the patio and slow dance to some favorite love songs that the two of you cherish.

Then lighten up the mood by moving to the family room where comedy awaits, and enjoy a video of your favorite comedian.

Conclude your evening by moving to the bathroom where a hot bubble bath awaits to assist in bringing closure to your entertainment tour.

Portable Hot Tub
♥

If you don't have the luxury of owning your own hot tub, you can make your own. Buy a sturdy, plastic children's pool that you can easily store and move around the house. Attach a garden hose to your sink by using an easy-to-find attachment and fill the pool to your desired temperature. Depending on the length of your hose and your faith in the leak-proof pool, you can move your portable hot tub to any room in the house.

Imagine the convenience you can have if you place the tub in the middle of the kitchen! You can reach all the beverages in the refrigerator, pull piping hot appetizers from the oven, and wash the dishes all while enjoying the lavishness of your portable hot tub.

Theme Baths
♥

Taking a bath together is a favorite activity for many couples. Instead of the traditional bubble bath you can add some variety by giving your next bath a theme.

For example, try a fruit theme. Surround the tub with different fruits. Use soap shaped like a pear. Fill the bathroom sink with crushed ice and have fruit juice cooling. If you get really silly you can always bob-for-apples.

Cushion Fort
♥

Before your wife comes home, use your childhood architecture skills. Rearrange the furniture and cushions in the living room and build a fort. Once your wife walks in the house, invite her to join you inside the fort for a time of talking, laughing, telling secrets that your parents can never find out, and eating nine peanut butter and jelly sandwiches.

If you have extra time, design your own internal communication system with two cans and string so you can talk to each other in case you're separated by a sudden cushion crash.

*G*arage Sale Vacation
♥

Cleaning the house isn't usually an event most couples look forward to. But the rewards of this particular activity may provide some extra motivation. The idea is to have a garage sale knowing that whatever money is raised will go toward a vacation.

Spend an entire day purging the house of items that are still in good condition but aren't being used. (This may produce some tension if something that appears to be junk to you has sentimental value to your spouse. Be sensitive!)

Obviously the romance isn't in the housecleaning, but in the aftermath of the sale as you dream, plan, and finally take your vacation. If the site of your vacation depends on how much money you make, you'd better brush up on your sales techniques. Otherwise, your holiday may start and end at a fast-food restaurant.

*D*rive-In Garage
♥

Rent a couple of your favorite videos and set up your television and VCR in the garage. Fill your car with munchies and a blanket and watch the movie from the front seat (or back seat—depending on your era) as if you were in a drive-in. Be sure to roll the windows down or you won't be able to hear—unless you have a convertible.

If you want to surprise your spouse, set everything up beforehand, blindfold her, drive around the city for awhile letting her think you're going somewhere else, and then return to the comforts of your garage. Be sure to take your remote control so you never have to leave the car. And don't keep your car engine running. If you do, not only will the movie be very short, but so will your life.

Miniature Golf Through the House

♥

Using plastic cups, you can create your own miniature golf course by placing the cups in different locations around the house. You'll need at least one putter and two golf balls. Make the holes as difficult or easy as you would like and invent rules and penalties to keep the game exciting. Remember that on most quality miniature golf courses the last hole is played for a prize.

If you're more romantic than competitive the prize could be a lot of fun.

If you're more competitive than romantic you might end up making your own boxing ring to settle the score.

Dream Come True

♥

Most couples dream about doing something fresh and exciting to their home or to specific rooms within the house. Spend time together dreaming about what you'd like to do someday to renovate your home. Put together a wish-list of what such an effort might entail. Don't place time expectations on fulfilling your dreams, but do outline some of the specific details needed in order to make the dream come true.

Once you've finished dreaming, file the ideas away. Then plan a weekend or a full day where the two of you work side-by-side to make the dream become a reality. There's a special feeling of accomplishment and camaraderie when you work together to bring a dream to life.

*H*eaven at Home
♥

You've probably seen movies depicting heaven with a cloudy or foggy atmosphere. You can create that same type of mood in your very own bedroom.

Invite your wife to a romantic date in your bedroom and explain to her that her presence will be like a "touch of heaven." Give her a specific time to meet you in the room so you'll have enough time to get the room prepared.

Here's what you'll need to make this happen: a five-gallon bucket, cardboard, blow dryer, a piece of dryer vent hose, and some dry ice (check Yellow Pages under ice).

Cut two holes in the cardboard—one hole for the nozzle of the blow dryer to fit through and the other hole for the hose. Half-fill the bucket with hot water, then cover the top of the bucket with the cardboard so that it fits snug over the bucket (you may need to use some duct tape for this). Put chopped pieces of the dry ice in the bucket (through one of the holes). After the ice is in, turn on the blow dryer and put it in its appropriate hole. (See illustration on the next page.)

The air from the blow dryer will force the fog out of the other hole or out of the vent hose that is placed through the other hole in the cardboard. The longer your vent hose, the more broadly you can spread the fog throughout your room.

Now that your room looks like heaven, you'll have to figure out what to do with the rest of your time.

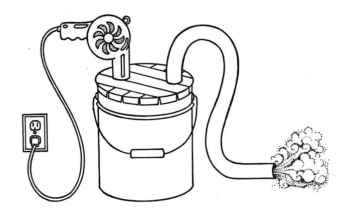

*C*ook with Me
♥

If your spouse doesn't know how to cook (like me!) plan a big dinner that he prepares. Your role as the expert chef is to stay in the kitchen and guide him through the process. Don't rescue him if he's having a difficult time but encourage him and—please—laugh *with* him rather than *at* him.

Now you must realize there's a small probability you will want to dine out after he's finished. As a matter of fact, if you can eat the food he has cooked, that will amount to the ultimate compliment.

(This idea can obviously work with either spouse since many husbands share the responsibility of cooking for the family—God bless them.)

*G*arage Party
♥

If your garage is clean you can quickly decorate it and turn it into a party room. Dream up a reason to give your spouse a party and prepare to celebrate. Use the normal trimmings: streamers, balloons, banners, etc. Once the garage is decorated you'll be ready to unleash the surprise at your convenience.

With a stereotypical surprise party, the unexpected happens the moment your surprised spouse walks through the door. With the garage party you can make the surprise happen whenever you want (especially if you're not dependent on waiting friends). The surprise can happen as soon as you ask him to empty the trash.

If the garage isn't clean, ask him to clean it out and then pull the surprise party later to reward his efforts. If he resents cleaning the garage altogether, forget the whole thing!

*B*ackyard Rain Forest
♥

If you don't have the time to leave the house for an adventurous trip you can create the next best thing by turning your backyard into a private rain forest. Set up a two-person tent on your grass and surround it with lots of plants. Add to the atmosphere by playing a sound track of animal noises or by putting the sprinkler on a mist setting somewhere in the background. Make dinner from food items you've packed into your backpack. Try to eat your meal through mosquito masks and then settle into your sleeping bags for a night of camping.

(If you don't like to "rough it" all that much, you can call this idea the "Backyard Hilton." Drag your television into the yard and then go sleep in the house once it gets too cold.)

Creative
Gift Giving

♥

10

*W*e sometimes give the impression that we don't like to receive gifts by the polite, social comments we utter before ripping the wrapping paper away—"You shouldn't have," or "I don't deserve this." The truth is, most of us love to get presents. It's a wonderful feeling when someone thinks we are special enough to spend time and money on. And the older we get, the more accurate mom's old adage becomes, "It's the thought that counts."

Once you've decided upon the "right" gift to buy, in this chapter you'll find some unique ways to present it to your husband or wife.

*D*id You Order This?

♥

If you want to give your spouse a gift at a restaurant, make arrangements in advance to take the gift to your server. When you arrive at the restaurant, you will already have arranged to have him present it on the dessert platter, on a large serving tray, in the bread basket, or with the change from the check. Allow the server some freedom and creativity so he will have fun helping you with your surprise. Servers are usually very willing to help out with these fun ideas.

By the way, don't allow romance to so overwhelm your sense of reality that you forget to leave a good tip.

*C*ar Shopping

♥

Suggest to your mate that you check out the latest cars at Harold's Used Cars. Arrange with Harold ahead of time to have the gift hidden in the trunk of one of the cars. As you browse through the cars, the salesman can suggest you check out the roominess of the trunk. When he opens the trunk the gift will stare the two of you in the face! If the car you are looking at is one he has been dreaming about for years he may want to use your gift as a down payment.

*C*leopatra

♥

This idea might work best after you've rented a

video of *The Land of the Pharoahs* or *Anthony and Cleopatra.* Then you'll be able to picture the setting: grapes, fans, a cool drink, and soft music. Set up a bed of comfort for your spouse. Serve her a refreshing beverage, fan her toward a restful mood and hand-feed her grapes or exotic fruits. Deliver her gifts during this pampering and feeding to add to the elegance of your Egyptian service.

*H*iding Out
♥

If you don't feel like you have time to set up some of the other ideas in this chapter, you can simply be creative by hiding your gift to be discovered in the course of a daily route. For example, a gift strategically hidden in the shrubs can be a great surprise on a hike or walk—"Hey, what's that red ribbon behind the eucalyptus?" Or you might hide a gift in your mate's office and call anonymously with a hint.

You'll find that even a simple element of surprise will give your gift greater meaning.

*S*tring 'Em Along
♥

A fun way to give a gift, big or small, extravagant or simple, is to create a trail through your home with string designed to lead your mate to the gift. Attach the string to the front door so that when she walks into the house she will know she's to begin following the string. You can leave smaller presents, notes, or little treats along the way, and wind the string all over your house in order to add creativity and suspense. This is a great way to make a small gift seem larger.

*F*or Your Eyes Only
♥

The following memo is a fun way to leave a clue that will lead your spouse to her hidden gift. If she hasn't seen this book you can use this word-for-word, and if she has seen it you can use it as a model to help in writing your own. (Be sure to insert your wife's name or we could both be in trouble—unless her name is Cathy Fields.)

Confidential Memo

To: Cathy Fields

From: Bond... Doug Bond

Re: Top Secret Box

Mission:
To locate and unwrap the secret box.

Your Task:

To travel throughout the house on your hands and knees in a relentless search to locate the box. Don't leave any cushion unturned or any cupboard closed. We have records of our last intelligence personnel, agent 009, who was unable to locate anything before she suddenly disappeared.

When you locate the box verify its contents with me by quickly calling me at the office and I'll give you further clues.

Good luck, Cathy. As always, memorize
and destroy this memo immediately.

Let's Make a Deal

♥

Place your gift under a box. Get two boxes of similar
size and place "loser" gifts under them (canned
food, an old pair of shoes, etc.). Allow your spouse to
choose one of the three boxes. If he chooses the wrong
box, show him his loser gift and grant him another
guess for performing a stunt or favor (a back rub, etc.).

If he chooses the right box on his first guess you can
either allow him to open the box or make him think
he's picked the wrong one and keep him guessing. If
you have a good poker face he'll continue questioning
his choices.

Stocking in July

♥

Locate the storage box containing your Christmas
supplies and find your spouse's stocking. Fill it
with gifts and hang it over the fireplace so she will see
it when she walks in the house. The surprise of seeing
the stocking in a month other than December may be
as much fun as the gifts.

Surprise Cereal

♥

Place your gift in the bottom of the your husband's favorite cereal. Act surprised when your small, wrapped

present plops into his bowl. (Hopefully he hasn't put the milk in the bowl first!)

Gifted Chore
♥

Prior to a "work day" around the house, hide your gifts in places your spouse will see as he prepares to do his work. For example, if his chores include washing the car and mowing the lawn, hide your gift with the washrags he'll use for the car or in the grass-catcher of the lawn mower.

Caution: If the gifts are too much fun he may not finish his chores.

Car Stop
♥

Lots of people I know use a hanging tennis ball to lightly rest against their car window inside the garage, so they know when they should stop the car. While your spouse is away, replace the tennis ball with a small, wrapped gift. She will be shocked when she enters the garage and finds a wrapped package resting against her window instead of the tennis ball.

Disguise a Friend
♥

Visit a thrift store and design a costume for one of your friends to wear to alter his usual appearance. During dinner or an important meeting have him enter in his disguise and deliver your wife's present. The shock of seeing him dressed as a mailman, police officer or Sumo wrestler will add to the delight of the gift.

Personalized Catalog
♥

Choosing items from colorful catalogs has always been a fun and convenient way to shop. You can make your own catalog by keeping a file of your spouse's wish-list items. If your spouse comments on something he sees advertised in a magazine, cut that page out and file it away. When he goes to the store and comments about how he wishes he could afford a particular "toy," grab anything that gives details on the toy and stick it away in the file. Continually be on the lookout for the items he desires.

Then, when you have enough photos, brochures, torn-out ads, etc., you can put together your own "Wish Book" filled with things you know he's interested in. This will make your gift-giving easier, and when you give the gift, you can let him know you picked it out of your own personal catalog. He will be thrilled that you took the time to keep track of his desires.

Silent Version of
Hot Versus Cold
♥

This creative way to give a gift is derived from the old hot/cold game played in elementary schools where the teacher hides something in the room while one of the students is waiting outside. When the student comes back in the room the other children shout "hot" if the student moves in the direction of the hiding place, or they shout "cold" if he heads in the wrong direction.

If you're an extrovert with lots of energy, here's how you can play a silent version of "hot/cold" with your spouse. Begin by hiding your gift. Then hand your spouse a clue sheet similar to the example on the next page. When she moves in the wrong direction you communicate "cold" by acting out one of the items under the "cold" category. Her job is to look on the clue sheet, find what you are acting out, and determine if her direction is hot or cold. If she begins moving in the right direction then you'll need to perform an action under the "hot" column. You can either photocopy the clue sheet provided or make up your own clues.

Hopefully, she will find the gift before you die of exhaustion.

Silent Hot Versus Cold
Clue Sheet

Hot

Jumping jacks
Shake your head indicating no
Spin in circles
Jump up and down
Scream
Stick your tongue out
Raise your hands above your head

Cold

Hop on one leg
Shake in convulsions
Do push-ups

Hop back and forth
Lick your lips
Blink your eyes
Laugh hysterically

Taking Romance on the Road

♥

11

*J*ust Go!

Vacations are an essential part of romantic marriage. They break our routines, inspire new thinking, and help us create joyful memories to sustain us through the tough times. The problem with vacations is that we don't go on them often enough. We've always got excuses to keep us from going. Someone once told me there is no good time to take a vacation.

However, I want to encourage you to get out and go! Not all vacations have to be expensive "biggies." Whether it's a trip to Sicily or a night in the city, it's time you blocked out some dates on your calendar. On the following pages you'll find a few creative vacation ideas and some suggestions to help you make your vacations both romantic and affordable.

*L*earning Vacation
♥

One of the most rewarding activities for couples is learning together. Yes, you read that right: learning together. Chances are, it was the catalyst for a romance or two during your own educational career. Maybe you even married your biology lab partner. If the smell of formaldehyde still puts stars in your eyes—or even if it doesn't—you can combine romance with learning and thus create a great lesson in love.

For example, you can spend a week at an archaeological dig, or five days on a working ranch, or two days reliving the battle of Gettysburg with a private guide. You can sign up for a weekend retreat throwing pottery, tackling conversational Japanese, exploring astronomy, or considering the migration of the California gray whale.

If you want to strike out on your own, take a driving trip to explore a subject that interests both of you: gardening, architecture, literature, music. Read together, quiz each other, stay up late, think new thoughts, and dream new dreams.

*B*icycle Touring
♥

Imagine viewing the countryside of Vermont or the Maine coastline in the course of a leisurely bicycle tour. In the afternoon, the guide leads you up the driveway to a country inn: Your evening is open—a hot shower, a wonderful meal, a beautiful private room till morning. After breakfast, you and the few other riders on the tour saddle up and pedal down the backroads to the next inn, waiting to give your body needed rest.

Such bicycle tours are offered by organizations in many locations around the country. Most offer various types of rides ranging from weekend jaunts to week-long treks. The rides are designed to be taken at a comfortable pace for any active adult. A "sag wagon" is even available if you get too pooped-to-pedal. Your luggage is transported for you, so you don't have to strap everything to your bike. And if you don't have a bike, the tour company will rent you one. (You can find listings for bicycle tours in the back of *Bicycling* and *Outside* magazines.)

House-Sitting
♥

One of the least expensive vacations available is staying at another family's house while they are on vacation. You provide them with the peace of mind that their home will be safe—no one likes to leave behind an empty house. They provide you with free accommodations.

Call friends and relatives who live in places you'd like to visit. Find out if and when they're going away, and offer to house-sit. If your home is in an area they might want to visit, you can even offer to swap houses.

Weekend Getaway
♥

Most hotels cater to business travelers who come and go during the week but leave behind halls of many hotels offer special weekend rates, which can be as low as half of the regular rate.

To lure couples from the local area, some of these hotels will provide breakfast with the room or offer a late check-out—in case you decide to sleep past noon.

When calling hotels to make a reservation, be sure to ask about some of the hidden costs—a $59 room can cost you $100 or more, depending on such things as these:

> *Room tax:* Cities can set their own rates, which sometimes go as high as 20 percent of the room rate.
>
> *Parking:* Most city hotels have garage parking that you'll have to pay for. And leaving your car on the street won't save you much money if it gets stolen.
>
> *Phone calls:* Many hotels charge 75¢ for a local call—not cheap if you're calling the baby-sitter every few hours.
>
> *Damages:* Let's say you're staying in room 723 and decide to have a barbecue in your room. For some reason the drapes catch fire and set off the sprinklers which pour 500 gallons of water into your room. The fire is extinguished, water rains into room 623 and disturbs a couple celebrating their twenty-fifth wedding anniversary. When the fire department arrives, they kick in the door of room 823 and interrupt a couple on their wedding night.
> You can be charged the cost of all fire and water damage, plus the cost of any counseling the newlyweds might require.

*C*ontrarian Vacation

♥

Suppose you take a week off from the bumper-to-bumper commute and wait an hour in line for a ride at Disney World. Or you're vacationing from your diet, but everything is so expensive you lose weight on the trip anyway. And you thought this vacation was a way to "get away from it all"!

Too many people going to the same places at the same time create problems of their own. And sometimes the problems are the very ones we harassed vacationers were trying to get away from: crowds, stress, lines, irritated people, and money worries.

The contrarian's vacation strategy is simple: If you want to travel to a popular place, go at an unpopular time. If you want to vacation at a popular time of year, choose an unpopular place.

Contrarians stay at ski resorts in the summer, beaches in the winter, go to New England in the spring, and the desert in the fall. They save so much money in off-season rates that they can afford more vacations. But their trips are so unstressful, they don't need to. They experience places in different ways and create memories unlike anyone else's.

If your vacations are causing you stress, be contrary.

*L*ocal Tourists

♥

It's strange but true—many people have never visited their own hometown. What I mean is, most people haven't seen the sites, taken the tours, and experienced their own communities the way an out-of-town vacationer would. Maybe it's time to change that.

For an inexpensive and jet-lagless weekend vacation, check into a local hotel. Pick up the brochures in the visitor's information rack and plan what you want to do. Try to find sites, restaurants, and tourist attractions you've never explored. If there's any kind of a historical or sightseeing tour, sign up. Take plenty of pictures, and don't forget to pick up postcards to send the folks "back home."

Note: If no one has ever vacationed in your town because it's just not that kind of town, then pick the nearest town that is.

*O*vernights

♥

Even if you're overscheduled and too low on cash to take a full-fledged vacation, perhaps you can manage an overnighter. These one-night vacations aren't adequate substitutes for several days of uninterrupted lounging, but they can help you catch your breath and reacquaint yourselves. Turn one of your date-nights into a once-a-month overnighter. Here are some options:

Show Time: Take in a show in the city, then stay at a hotel.

Starry Starry Night: Pack sleeping bags and a plastic tarp. Drive to a campground, pull out the gear, pull up the covers, and count the stars.

Bed and Breakfast: Stay one night. Go for an evening stroll and an early morning walk. Eat a big breakfast.

Surprise Attack: Meet him for dinner, take him to a hotel, unpack his pajamas, hang up the "Do Not Disturb" sign.

Storybook Break: Rent a cabin with a fireplace. Unplug the phone, the TV, the radio. Read a children's classic aloud. Fall asleep in front of the fire, then pick up the story again at breakfast.

In-Flight Meal
♥

If airline food is so bad, why do we eat it? Peer pressure. You don't want to eat it, but as the flight attendants carry the trays down the aisle to less discriminating passengers, the odor drifts past you and you think, "That doesn't really smell bad..." Everyone else has decided to dine, so you take a tray, peel off the plastic, fold back the foil, and taste the meal. Then you realize that peer pressure and cabin pressure are somehow connected, because you wouldn't be eating that stuff at ground level.

So what does this have to do with vacations? Well, if your trip starts with a plane flight, you can stand up to the peer pressure together without going hungry. On most airlines, you can request a special meal when you make your reservations. You may be able to order a vegetarian, seafood, low calorie, or fruit meal—your travel agent can tell you what's available. Because these meals are specially prepared, they tend to taste better. So instead of eating what was prepared for you and 40,000 other people that day, you can treat yourselves to something prepared for a mere hundred other nonconformists.

*H*otel Picnics

♥

One of the most expensive aspects of a hotel stay is the food bill. A continental breakfast can cost $10 and a simple late-night snack from room service will probably add up to at least $15. Here's a way to beat the high prices and create some fun:

First of all, when you're packing for the trip, squeeze in two settings of picnic plates, bowls, and tableware, and add a sharp knife.

When you arrive at your hotel, go to a nearby market and buy a Styrofoam ice chest (usually less than $5). Stock it with whatever you want, and at the same time pick up other nonperishable snacks. (Of course, if you're driving to your destination, you can bring your own ice chest and do your grocery shopping at home.)

Back in your hotel room, fill the chest with ice from the machine down the hall, and pack the perishables inside it. Now when you get hungry for a snack or light meal, you don't have to get sick over the price.

*R*oom Snacks and Meals

> *Captain Crunch bed:* Pick up small boxes of your favorite childhood cereal and serve yourselves breakfast in bed. If it's Saturday, lie around in your pajamas all morning and watch cartoons. (Don't forget the "Do Not Disturb" sign!)

> *Pack-a-snack:* If you'll be touring points of interest all day, prepare a snack to bring with you like crackers and sliced cheese, grapes, apple slices, and juice boxes.

Cold and bubbly: Chill down a bottle of your own, serve it whenever and wherever you like.

Bridge lunch: If you eat a big breakfast that is provided with the room and plan to have a fancy dinner, you can prepare simple sandwiches for lunch. This will carry you through the between time—and save you money for the night's meal.

Milk and cookies: Have a tall glass of cold milk and a handful of your favorite cookies. Eat them in bed, on the floor, in the tub— there's nothing your mom can do to stop you.

Ice cream melt: Unless you're some sort of cryogenic genius, you won't be able to keep ice cream frozen in your ice chest very long. Who cares? Serve it anyway, partially melted and oozing from the container, sprinkled with crumbled Reese's Peanut Butter Cups or Ovaltine powder. This is what vacations are for.

*R*eentry Day
♥

Most couples plan their vacations to end the night before they're due back in the "real world." Instead of being rejuvenated Monday morning, they're tired, stressed from the rush to get home, and wishing they had some time off to recover from their vacation. On your next trip, plan to come home a day early. Here's what you can do on your reentry day.

♥ Sleep in. There's no bed like home.

♥ Eat a normal, cheap breakfast. No more hotels ($4.50 for a glass of orange juice) or

   airplanes ($298 roundtrip for soggy eggs).

♥ Drop off the film to be developed.

♥ Unpack. Make a list of all the things you packed but never used and make a vow never to overpack again.

♥ Do the laundry. Scrape the mud off your shoes ("Trust me, honey—this is a short-cut..."), take the blouse to the dry cleaner ("And I'll have barbecued ribs..."), and put the hem back in the trousers ("Let's dance!").

♥ Gather all the credit card receipts, but don't look at them until the next day at work: This will motivate you to ask for a raise to pay for them.

♥ Send all the postcards you bought but didn't have stamps for.

That evening, while everyone else on vacation is fighting traffic or filling out lost-luggage claims at the airport, you'll be snuggling at home, reminiscing about your trip—and planning the next one.

Keep vacationing!

The Power of Words

♥

12

William James, the father of American psychology, once said the deepest desire in human nature is the craving to be appreciated. In my ministry as well as in my personal life, I know this is true. We have an almost insatiable need to be approved for being who we are.

The moment we entered this world as infants, we required physical attention and other forms of affection. And that same basic human desire for encouragement helps build our feelings of appreciation for each other as adults.

I value the affirmation and applause of others after giving a speech or while working on a project. But I find few things more rewarding than the verbal appreciation of my wife. Yes, I want to be acknowledged as her husband, and I need to be accepted as her husband. However there is incredible satisfaction when I am valued by her as a person—a person who also happens to be her husband.

It's no secret that discouragement and pessimism thrive in our society. One of today's most familiar tragedies is that people are sharing their daily lives with the one person who could meet their emotional needs, and yet the encouraging words they so want to hear are simply never spoken.

Millions of men and women live out the majority of their years unfulfilled by their spouses. How tragic!

The words we choose to use when communicating with our spouses can make or break the very foundations of our relationships. Positive words express appreciation and build up the other person. Harmful words tear apart our sense of worth, and force our relational foundations to crumble. You hold, with your choice of words, the ability to gravely wound your spouse, or to help him or her live a more joyful and vivacious life.

Instead of pacifying your spouse's need with occasional encouragement, I want to challenge you to do more. Try to implement these three action steps, which will start you on the road toward expressing the type of appreciation that really satisfies.

*A*ction #1:
Weigh Your Words
♥

As a child I memorized a trite cliche to counteract my verbal abusers on the playground. It went like this: "Sticks and stones may break my bones but words will never hurt me." It's a cute saying—quick, melodic, and easy to remember. But it's far from being an accurate description of reality. The person who wrote it was either a fool or was quite unaware of the destructive impact words can have on our vulnerable feelings. Personally, I'd rather be hit with a stick than take verbal punishment.

Words hurt! Ugly words directed toward another person have the ability to disfigure their emotional features. The Bible refers to the tongue as a small part of the body that has potential for great evil. Unfortunately, we often spew out evil and damaging words as ammunition when we are hurt, when we become defensive, or when we become angry.

Later on, although we may regret our words and plead forgiveness, the spoken word has already lodged in the heart of the receiver and may never be forgotten. Negative words last far beyond the quick breath we use to say them.

I challenge you to weigh the words you speak to your spouse (as well as others) knowing they may cause great harm. Be reminded by the wisdom of this proverb: "What you say affects how you live. You will be rewarded by how you speak. What you say can mean life or death" (Proverbs 18:20,21).

*A*ction #2:
Be Generous with Compliments
♥

Your spouse is worthy of your generous approval. Don't feel like you must be frugal in your spending of good words. Good words build and motivate, and I've yet to meet anyone suffering from overencouragement. Chances are high you're surrounded by people who are malnourished from a lack of positive input, and need someone who isn't afraid to be lavish in their giving of words.

When you are being liberal with praise it doesn't have to happen only behind closed doors. When you compliment your husband or wife in the presence of others, it amounts to a double blessing.

*A*ction #3:
Perform Heart Surgery
♥

Jesus tells us that our words and actions reflect the condition of our hearts. What types of words are coming from your mouth? If you have an easier time being sarcastic, critical and negative than you do at being uplifting and positive, you may need to perform heart surgery on yourself.

This is a painful step because it involves internal reflection. Nevertheless, the words of Christ are fairly direct and self-explanatory, "The mouth speaks the things that are in the heart. A good person has good things in his heart..." (Matthew 12:34,35).

If you're like me, this is a really tough principle to swallow. I usually speak before I think, and the condition of my heart becomes all too obvious. At times of confrontation or irritation, it's much easier to say cutting and hurtful words than words of genuine love. Is this the case with you?

Heart surgery means asking tough questions of yourself about the types of words that come from your mouth. It also means examining what fills your life and heart. Jesus speaks about this in the context of good and bad trees. He says, "If you want good fruit, you must make the tree good. If your tree is not good, then it will have bad fruit. A tree is known by the kind of fruit it produces" (Matthew 12:33).

Your marriage can't grow if you're not producing good fruit. You may need to ask God to do some pruning on your life so the bad fruit can shrivel up and fall off and leave plenty of room for good fruit. God is more than willing to help you with the surgery, but you need to acknowledge the need for it.

Your spouse is an incredible gift from God. People are precious gifts, and we should make them feel valued by choosing words that build them up. Remember, brick by brick, word by word, you're building a great cathedral.

Here are some words to reflect upon. Think them through, one by one, as you begin to keep your commitment toward encouragement.

compassion	encouraging
caring	humorous
listening	direct
trustworthy	sympathetic
loyal	cheerful
organized	helpful
creative	spiritual
nurturing	sincere
humble	confident
optimistic	cooperative
giving	courteous
faithful	decisive
forgiving	flexible
sensitive	patient
perceptive	energetic
persevering	friendly
visionary	respectful

Now that you've given some thought to those concepts, here are a few phrases to consider. This is by no means an exhaustive list, but it should give you some ideas about the kinds of words spouses like to hear from each other.

Women love to hear their husbands say...

♥ What can I do to help?

♥ I really want to understand what you're feeling.

♥ I'd marry you all over again in a minute!

♥ Thank you!

♥ I was wrong. I'm very sorry.

♥ I'm the luckiest person alive to have you as my wife.

♥ You look very beautiful...you *are* very beautiful.

♥ What do you think about...? (Value her opinion.)

♥ I love being with you.

♥ You are the prettiest person in this room.

♥ I really care.

♥ I admire the way you care for our children.

Men want to hear things like this:

♥ Thank you for working so hard!

♥ I feel really safe when I'm with you.

♥ You turn me on!

♥ If only my friends had husbands like you.

♥ You're a great father.

♥ I could watch you all day!

♥ I appreciate the way you handled that situation.

♥ Can I do something to help relieve your stress?

♥ When you do that (say that, act that way, etc.) it really makes me feel loved.

♥ I thought about you all day and couldn't wait to see you.

*C*reative
Entertainment

♥

13

I've said it once, and I'll say it again—you don't have to be an expert in sociology, theology, or psychology to understand the simple truth that people crave appreciation. Our human nature requires it—everyone longs to be appreciated! Meanwhile criticism, coldness, and cynicism pollute our attitudes and distort our hopes.

True encouragement actually affirms the worth and dignity that God wants His children to feel. In this chapter, I hope you'll find ideas that will help you encourage your mate. Your spouse needs your encouragement. And the effects of your personal inspiration can be life-changing.

Encouragement Calendar

♥

Place a stack of 3 x 5 index cards in areas where you spend a great deal of your time (car, office, kitchen, etc.). When you think of something that you appreciate about your spouse, write the affirmation on an index card. In addition to words of appreciation you might write personal comments that would be positive and fun to read.

When you have written 30 ideas, punch two holes in the top of the cards and bind them together with yarn. Put the stack on your spouse's desk so she will have your daily encouragement for a month.

Valentines on Sale

♥

On the first few days following Valentine's Day you can buy beautiful cards and Valentine paraphernalia at half price. Load up on a supply of discounted "love-thoughts." You'll be able to keep the romance of Valentine's Day alive all year long.

Making the News

♥

Nothing would please your mate more than reading the morning paper and finding a professional ad with a love note from you. Placing an ad in the local paper is an easy way to say "I love you," and it will stick in his memory longer than the sports page headlines.

If you're feeling creative and wealthy you can buy a full-page ad. This whole page can be filled with photos, quotes from your relationship, poems, and inside jokes, as well as your loving encouragement.

You will be surprised at how inexpensive advertising space is in some of the smaller community papers.

*B*aby's Way
♥

This childish way to encourage can easily be done if you have one of those portable monitor systems used to supervise the baby's sleep noises. When your spouse is near the speaker you can sneak into your baby's room and speak to your mate over the intercom. It becomes humorous at first because of the shock but as your spouse hears your encouraging words, compliments, and reasons why you love her she may not make you change diapers for a week.

*T*he Great Interrupter
♥

Imagine this scene: You're sitting with your mate eating leftovers, engaged in conversation about the day's events, and your spouse suddenly interrupts your conversation and says, "You are beautiful!" After saying this he walks around the table (or crawls over the table!) and kisses you.

Catch your spouse by surprise by interrupting the normal routine and expressing the wonderful truth you feel deep inside. Your mate will never be more happy to be interrupted! Startle your husband by telling him why you're glad you married him, what you love about his looks, how he makes you feel special, and how you'd fall in love with him in a minute if you had your life to live all over again.

*H*allmark Bill
♥

Most normal people hate receiving monthly bills, but they do welcome fun cards—especially the ones with personal messages from their beloved. You can bring some delight to the boring task of paying bills by inserting a humorous card into the monthly pile of debts. This depressing time can become exciting when your mate finds a thoughtful card signed by an encouraging spouse. The final total in the checking account won't get any less, but your husband or wife may begin to look forward to the end of the month anyway.

*P*ocket Talk
♥

Surprise your mate by placing an encouraging note in her pocket before she leaves for work. By leaving notes in the pockets of pants, jackets, blouses, and sweaters, you'll condition your spouse to become a "pocket searcher" for your kind words. You may find that your note will go unnoticed for a few weeks, which will delay your encouragement but won't lessen the impact.

*P*hone Machines
♥

While many people view phone answering machines as a nuisance, you can use yours as an assistant in leaving your encouraging messages. Leave your affirming words while your spouse is out of the house. When she returns to check her messages she will be interrupted by a pleasant surprise. Though this sounds like a simple idea, you'll be amazed at how your continual and uncomplicated words of love will astound your spouse. If you really want to shock her, leave a dozen different messages, each one expressing your love.

*V*iva la Video
♥

Use a video camera to interview some of the people closest to your wife or husband. Record them as they tell you what they like most about your mate. Ask the people to condense their thoughts to approximately two minutes—this will keep them from babbling and will make the video more pleasant to view.

Surprise your spouse by putting in your homemade video when he's expecting to watch the next rental movie. Your camera work may not challenge the professional quality of Hollywood, but he will remember the kind words and your effort a lot longer than any movie's plot.

*T*ime Capsule
♥

Build your own time capsule by taking a piece of plastic PVC pipe and enclosing it with two end caps. A small item or a personal letter is the perfect gift to put inside the pipe. Then seal it with the caps.

Decorate the PVC pipe with paints or permanent markers. For true authenticity you might include a silicon gel packet, which you can purchase at a hobby store, to remove the humidity. Bury your capsule and provide clues or a map so the capsule will be found.

If your map isn't accurate, your gift may become the treasure of another generation.

*W*orking for Worth
♥

Design your next letter of encouragement to be a mystery by calculating a code that must be "cracked" before your spouse discovers the thoughtful message. Here's an example of what I mean:

A = 1	J = 10	S = 19
B = 2	K = 11	T = 20
C = 3	L = 12	U = 21
D = 4	M = 13	V = 22
E = 5	N = 14	W = 23
F = 6	O = 15	X = 24
G = 7	P = 16	Y = 25
H = 8	Q = 17	Z = 26
I = 9	R = 18	

9   23 1 14 20   25 15 21   20 15   11 14 15 23
20 8 1 20   9 ' 4   16 12 1 25   1 14 25   7 1 13 5
20 15   5 24 16 18 6 19 19   13 25   12 15 22 5
20 15   25 15 21.

(Answer: I want you to know that I'd play any game to express my love to you.)

*S*urprise Page
♥

This fun idea will work when you're at a restaurant that uses an intercom paging system. Excuse yourself to go to the restroom. On your way, stop at the front desk and give the host your encouraging message for your mate. Ask the host to page your spouse a few minutes after you've returned to your table. When your wife arrives at the host's station she will be shocked to receive her encouraging message from a stranger.

*C*artoon Rewrite
♥

Photocopy a cartoon strip from a newspaper or comic book and cut out the original captions. Then write your own captions and personalize a love story that fits both your spouse and the cartoon. The creativity of the idea and the originality of your words will be a delightful surprise for your spouse and will remind her of your love when it hangs on the refrigerator.

*L*et the
Neighbors Know
♥

Hanging huge banners on the garage door seems to be an accepted form of communicating important messages. I've seen banners that say things like "Welcome Home," "It's a Boy!" and "Happy Birthday." This medium of communication is the perfect opportunity for you to share an encouraging message with your spouse . . . as well as the rest of the neighborhood.

Imagine the traffic jam in front of your house, with motorists reading your signs:

♥ | I Love You

♥ | You're the Best Wife in the World

♥ | I Was Wrong—I'm Sorry

- Welcome Home, Brilliant Husband
- Happy Anniversary
- I Love the Way You Make Me Feel

I Love You Pizza
♥

Next time you call in your pizza order, ask them to bake your special message into the cheese. A good pizza maker can write "I Love You" with pepperoni or olives, and underline words with green peppers. Obviously, your personal message can't be too long, but even a short note will surprise and please your spouse.

*W*alk of Fame
♥

In Hollywood, California, there are blocks of sidewalk that have been designated as the "Walk of Fame." Embedded cement stars are special awards given to well-loved personalities in the entertainment business. Not only is it a big honor for the star, but when a new star is unveiled, the media and fans show up to honor the celebrity and enjoy the festivities.

You can create your own walk of fame for your spouse. Paint, outline in tape, or chisel (be sure you aren't breaking a city ordinance!) a star in your sidewalk and put your spouse's name in it. Invite her friends to be the fans. You may even want to let the local newspaper know you're having a ceremony to honor the greatest star you know.

——— ♥ ———

My favorite books are short and practical. And so, with that tribute to your favorite star, I've said all I have to say for now. You're on your own!

As I noted before, this book wasn't written to provide you with "all the answers," but simply to give you enough new concepts to get you started. I'm not trying to sell books when I say, "If you apply just one idea from this book it may be worth the price you paid." I really believe it! If you are serious about romancing your spouse, now you have some innovative suggestions. Perhaps you've been challenged, too—challenged to love your spouse like a king or a queen.

The reality of broken families and painful relationships bears witness to the fact that building healthy marriages is difficult. My prayer is that you are now just a bit better prepared to provide your marriage with the life, laughter, and romance you and your spouse so richly deserve.

Your Romantic Location Could Be Worth $500

If you have a favorite romantic location you think is worth sharing, send it to me. I may print it in my future book, *Romantic Spots Across the Country*. If I use your location in my book, I'll send you a few bucks and give you credit for it. If I select your special place as the most romantic idea in the book, I'll send you $500!

Send in this form with your idea. Be sure to explain the setting and atmosphere as clearly as possible. Please give specific directions to your special place. By the way, you can send in as many ideas as you like.

Name _____

Address _____

City _____ St/Prov _____ Zip/Post _____

I'm submitting the attached romantic location for possible publication in Doug's future book, *Romantic Spots Across the Country*. To my knowledge, the publication of the attached idea/location will not violate any copyright belonging to someone else. I understand that if my idea is published, I'll receive payment—the amount to be determined by the author of the book, and payable upon publication.

Signature _____ Date _____

Send to:

DOUG FIELDS
P.O. Box 8329
Newport Beach, CA 92658

Other Good Harvest House Reading

TOO OLD, TOO SOON
by *Doug Fields*

Too Old, Too Soon examines the changes to childhood brought about by a culture caught in overdrive and offers concrete suggestions parents can use to avoid the pitfalls of rushing their children to adulthood.

FOR LOVERS ONLY
by *Stephen Schwambach*

This may be the most powerfully persuasive book ever written to convince a hard-hearted partner to call off the divorce and give his or her marriage one more try. Sixty short, powerful chapters illuminate the thinking of a stubborn spouse and provide direction for getting back on track.

ROMANTIC LOVERS
The Intimate Marriage
by *David and Carole Hocking*

Here is romantic love for married couples that exceeds our greatest dreams and expectations! Greater intimacy is possible as we follow God's beautiful picture of marriage as found in the Song of Solomon.

MARRIAGE PERSONALITIES
by *David Field*

Take a fresh look at marriage and its seven distinct personalities. Valuable information about marriage, new insights into your spouse's behavior, and an increased ability to give and receive deeper dimensions of love and joy.

QUIET TIMES FOR COUPLES
by *H. Norman Wright*

Noted counselor and author Norm Wright provides the help you need to nurture your oneness in Christ. In a few moments together each day you will discover a deeper, richer intimacy with each other and with God, sharing your fondest dreams and deepest thoughts—creating memories of quiet times together.

Dear Reader:

We would appreciate hearing from you regarding this Harvest House nonfiction book. It will enable us to continue to give you the best in Christian publishing.

1. What most influenced you to purchase *Creative Romance*?
   - ☐ Author
   - ☐ Subject matter
   - ☐ Backcover copy
   - ☐ Recommendations
   - ☐ Cover/Title
   - ☐ _____

2. Where did you purchase this book?
   - ☐ Christian bookstore
   - ☐ General bookstore
   - ☐ Department store
   - ☐ Grocery store
   - ☐ Other

3. Your overall rating of this book:
   ☐ Excellent ☐ Very good ☐ Good ☐ Fair ☐ Poor

4. How likely would you be to purchase other books by this author?
   - ☐ Very likely
   - ☐ Somewhat likely
   - ☐ Not very likely
   - ☐ Not at all

5. What types of books most interest you?
   (check all that apply)
   - ☐ Women's Books
   - ☐ Marriage Books
   - ☐ Current Issues
   - ☐ Self Help/Psychology
   - ☐ Bible Studies
   - ☐ Fiction
   - ☐ Biographies
   - ☐ Children's Books
   - ☐ Youth Books
   - ☐ Other _____

6. Please check the box next to your age group.
   - ☐ Under 18
   - ☐ 18-24
   - ☐ 25-34
   - ☐ 35-44
   - ☐ 45-54
   - ☐ 55 and over

Mail to: Editorial Director
Harvest House Publishers
1075 Arrowsmith
Eugene, OR 97402

Name _____

Address _____

City _____ State _____ Zip _____

Thank you for helping us to help you in future publications!